Talking

Stalking

Writing for Recovery

"Why write? To shine a light; to right a wrong; to shape chaos into art; to know what we think; to pose difficult questions; to challenge our own beliefs; to connect. Because we have to."

— *Dani Shapiro*

Veritas
Training · Research · Reform · Support

Writing Group Facilitator: Sam Taylor

Editing Team: Anusree Biswas Sasidharan, Nick Podd, Claudia Miles and Sam Taylor

Creative Design Work: (cover and formatting) Nick Podd

Researchers: Claudia Miles and Sam Taylor

Published 2015 Writing for Recovery Group University of Brighton, East Sussex

Printed by One Digital

ISBN number: 978-1-910172-07-0

This book is dedicated to all those who have tragically lost their lives at the hands of their stalkers and to those who have survived and continue to rebuild their lives despite the devastating effects of their experience.

We must not give up hope but rather continue sharing knowledge, working together and saving lives.

TABLE OF CONTENTS

Foreword

Stalking and harassment are crimes that have some of the biggest impact on their victims of any that the police deal with. They often have a debilitating effect, in part because they are usually perpetrated by someone who knows their victim: their movements, habits, likes and dislikes, their friends and their family, their strengths and weaknesses and their fears. Not many crimes have the potential to be so invasive, all consuming and destructive. In my twenty years as a police officer, I have seen this first hand on many occasions, and I am acutely aware of the very significant risks these crimes can pose to their victims and their families.

We are better now - as a society and as a police service - at recognising stalking and the impact and dangers posed by domestic abuse than we were, even five years ago. New laws specifically aimed at tackling stalking were introduced on 25th November 2012 and I was proud to see Sussex Police being the first force to be awarded White Ribbon status as part of the 'men ending violence towards women' campaign in July 2013. The thing is, that neither of these things would have been possible or achieved were it not for the support, help, strength and determination of survivors. Yes: *survivors* of some truly terrible, sometimes life-changing experiences have come back stronger, and become a force for change. I thank them and I admire them.

This book details some of their stories and it is impossible not to be moved by many of them.

I am regularly upset, angered and also inspired by the stories of domestic abuse and stalking that I hear day to day from my officers and staff describing cases that they are involved in. I am upset by the effect on the survivors and sometimes those close to them including children; angered by the destructive acts perpetrated by controlling selfish individuals and inspired by the determination, commitment and passion of officers and staff (often working closely with partner agencies), to intervene and to get justice. Most of all officers and staff in their support of survivors; I thank them too.

This book details the stories of survivors and the professionals involved in supporting them. Written by those who have survived and had the strength to tell their stories and some of the professionals working on the front-line; it is impossible not to be moved by them. I hope that the act of recording these stories and the creative energy behind that process has been cathartic for the people who have written them. I hope that it has reminded the professionals of how important and positively life-changing their work can be. Finally, I hope that this book will help you, as a reader, better understand stalking and its terrible consequences.

Nev Kemp
Sussex Police Commander for Brighton and Hove

Editor's Notes

This anthology was developed from the *Writing For Recovery* course run by Veritas Justice Director, Sam Taylor. As a member of the team I was keen to gain a better understanding of how Veritas worked with survivors of Stalking and professionals so I joined the groups. I witnessed first-hand how Sam expertly steered the group through various exercises and therapeutic techniques that brought the group together with moments of contemplation, reflection and quite often laughter. I also observed how Claudia Miles, our Legal Director, provided much needed no-nonsense advice on how to navigate within the family court system. I watched how Veritas Justice provided a comprehensive and flexible approach to supporting victims of stalking. The group context was especially valuable in combatting the sense of isolation that was felt by many of those attending the writing group.

This year of listening to accounts of stalking has shown me how commonplace stalking is within and outside domestic violence and in fact, how common it is to know one's stalker and how intimate and specific stalking can be. Stalkers can have a variety of motivations and techniques to interfere with the victim reflecting the challenges in previous legislation in prosecuting this crime. The new legislation attempts to capture the elusiveness of this crime and indeed the impact it has on its victim thus acknowledging not only violence but fear, serious alarm and distress.

This collection has resulted from these sessions over the past year, which involved both historic as well as ongoing stalking. At its foundation, this anthology seeks to explore the journeys of truly inspiring writers who through their creative development have produced some powerful work which shines a light on the darkness surrounding stalking and stalkers through having the courage to explore their own experiences and share. The contributors are a combination of those who have experienced stalking first-hand, those who observed either stalking and/or the impact of stalking, professionals and in some cases a combination. I want to particularly thank the anonymous contributors, whose writing apart from being beautifully written displayed a kind of honesty and poignancy that comes with anonymity. Together the collection has made this anthology that much richer and made sure that marginalised narratives were heard. Thank you.

The accounts given in the collection can often pose difficult questions, give valuable insights into the impact of stalking and expresses experiences often on the fringes of our understanding. Through film scripts, poetry, diary entries, prose and song lyrics this collection bears witness to the lives, relationships and portraits of what it means to live, write and survive.

Dr Anusree Biswas Sasidharan
Editor

A Message from Veritas Justice CIC

Veritas Justice is a community interest organisation working to raise awareness on the issues of Stalking, highlighting the importance of effective multi-agency work aimed at supporting victims whilst holding perpetrators to account.

Our unique approach combines legal, therapeutic and academic skills to train and support individuals and organisations alike.

We have been privileged to work with a group of passionate professionals, students and survivors in the production of this book working together to challenge the devastating effects of stalking and tackle the pervasive discourses of minimisation of victims experiences and mother blaming so often displayed in media reports which ignore the significance of the personal experiences thereby justifying the unacceptable.

We have learned how sharing knowledge can generate new ways of thinking about issues that greatly affect our community and the important contribution of the personal narratives as a valid form of knowledge.

We would like to thank all of our participants for sharing a wealth of knowledge with us. You have been truly inspiring!

We are also in debt to Dr Alec Grant for his continued support, advice and faith in us. Thanks Alec!

Thank you to the Veritas team who have supported us and worked with us to make this book a reality, despite the endless challenges – you know who you are!

Sam Taylor and Claudia Miles
Directors

HOUSE OF LORDS – 24th April 2012
Baroness Royall of Blaisdon:

My Lords, today we are almost there: a **new law on stalking**, for which Parliament rather than Government has been in the driving seat. Over the past six months, a staggering amount of progress has been made, much of it due to the advocacy of **noble Lords on all Benches.** Like the Minister, I pay special tribute to the noble Baroness, Lady Brinton, and the noble Baroness, Lady Howe, along with my noble friends on these Benches. The progress is also **testament to the campaigners**, the excellent parliamentary inquiry, and most of all to the survivors and their families that we will soon achieve proper protection in law for the victims of stalking. I also pay tribute to those women who have shown extraordinary courage in the face of this harrowing crime: **women like Claire Waxman, Tracey Morgan, Sam Taylor, Tricia Bernal and Claudia Miles,** whose lives were stolen by their stalkers, but all of whom are utterly determined to make sure that future victims get the justice and protection that they deserve.

The new Law for stalking was introduced on
25th November, Protection of freedoms and Punishment of
offenders Act 2012 after only ten months of campaigning.

Introduction

The idea of Writing for Recovery emerged for me after the publication of a collection of mental health service user and survivor narratives I had the pleasure of co-editing (Grant et al., 2011). Biographical writing in the service of self-exploration and self-development is by no means a new notion, as testified by the confessional writings of St. Augustine and Jean-Jaques Rousseau in the 4th and 18th centuries respectively. In our times, it has been used extensively in the context of the emergence of the 'narrative turn' in the social and human sciences, to celebrate reflexive, subjective, first person accounts as both research and therapeutic resources. In working in this area, I have been one of a number of applied scholars who both supports and role models the idea that we can all 're-story' ourselves through writing about our lives, both in terms of what has gone wrong in them and our wishes for the future (Grant and Zeeman, 2012).

Writing ourselves into the future is an important ethical act to make sense of our pasts, presents, and as yet unrealised but wished-for possibilities, and I have been proud to lead this form of practice development locally. Recent work has involved using these ideas to help mental health service users, carers and survivors in the recovery process (Taylor et al., 2014). It has also given me great pleasure to support the transfer of these initiatives to help victims of stalking. In this context, am proud to be associated with the excellent Veritas Justice organisation led by Sam and Claudia, and I commend this new collection to you.

Alec Grant, PhD
Reader in Narrative Mental Health
School of Health Sciences
University of Brighton

References:

Grant A, Biley F, Walker F (eds). 2011. *Our Encounters with Madness.* Ross-on-Wye: PCCS Books.

Grant AJ, Zeeman L. 2012. Whose Story Is It? An autoethnography concerning narrative identity. *The Qualitative Report (TQR).* 17:1-12.

Taylor S, Leigh-Phippard H, Grant A. 2014. Writing for Recovery: a practice development project for mental health service users, carers and survivors. *International Journal of Practice Development.* 14: 1-13.

WRITING FOR RECOVERY GROUP POEM

Anxiety, awaken, awkward
Battered, brutal, bastard
Constant, censored, connected, cyber, crap
Devious, darkness, danger,
Escape, every day, endless,
Frustrated, failed, fearful, fixated
Grandiose, go away, Gemini
Horror, hated, humiliation, hunted
Insomnia, injustice, injured, ironic
Joke, Jury, Justice
Killing, knotted, known
Lies, lame, lottery
Motherhood, misunderstood, misguided, misogyny
Narcissistic, nagging, never-ending, nightmare
Obsession, observed, obliged
Paranoid, perpetrator, privacy, permanent, psychopathy
Quit, qualified, quarrelsome, questionable
Rant, rude, running, restless
Surveillance, stop, support, sociopathic
Tantrum, time, taboo, taken
Untenable, underestimated, undeniable, unrealistic
Violated, violent, vicious, vain
Willing, weirdo, words, waste
X-ray, x-rated
Yield, you
Zero, zig-zag

Songs of

Experience

And his dark secret love

Does thy life destroy

— William Blake (Taken from Sick Rose in *Songs of Experience)*

Approximately 5 million people are stalked every year in the UK

British Crime Survey, 2009-12

The Shadow

Let me tell you a story, with a start but no end,
A tale of two girls so cruelly left to fend.

The start was so innocent, people said he was nice
But for believing this, these two did pay the price.

A drink in a bar, a meal in a house,
And suddenly BAM, a feeling of something else.

Slowly it seemed a shadow did grow,
Physically hidden but in my gut I did know.

Unfortunate events anxiously laughed away,
A huge bunch of flowers in the garden, left to lay.

Never to realise it had become so out of hand
Only later to find what he really had planned.

Then came the day, the chat on the road,
The opening of doors, unaware of what he had stowed.

Suddenly then a rough push to the floor
All freedom gone with the slam of that door.

A scream falling on an empty street
The sickening way a heart quickens its beat.

The pleadings of innocence and the cry of fear
Hopelessly falling on just a deaf ear.

The glints of a blade and the dark red of blood
Forever ingrained, never forgot.

Then enters a friend more innocent still
Just lighting his passion of which is to kill.

Flashbacks of a bath diluted with blood
The sound of her screams as his boot lands with a thud.

No reason is given for all of this pain
Just a desire to control a girl he couldn't once gain.

The moment of death we saw as so near
Covered in petrol and lying in fear.

To hug one another was our last resort
As the matches were flicked and so nearly caught.

Through weariness came a thought in the dark
A desperate lie on which we must embark.

The shadow soon ran so cowardly away
Leaving behind a night soon to become day.

For us to then run into a strangers embrace
The blanket of safety so gently placed.

The shadow was caught, guilty of all
But living through others, as for his innocence they call.

That nightmare may have ended, but still it will take
more
Before the shadow is no longer lurking at my door

To the weight that lives on my chest

To the weight that lives on my chest and deadens my
bones
And rings in my ear like a foreboding drone.

It's taken me time and talking and tears to figure out
finally what's fuelled you these years. And knowledge is
power; yes that's what they say,
So I'm finding a voice to engage you in play.
Play: a mad dance between hope and regret
Between what's done is done and the best lives in yet.

I'm stalking you now, each move you make.
And even if my bones hurt from rejection and hate,
I'm steeling myself.

For I choose to live and to dance and be free,
I'm choosing a different path,
I'm choosing me.

Time is no healer

Fifteen years on
And I find it hard to come to terms
With the fact
That I'm still afraid to answer the
Phone
In my own safe house
Instead
I let the answer machine be my voice
It's my shield
From your hateful noise

I sometimes wonder
Do you have the faintest idea
Just how much your vile, self-obsessed screeching
And monotonous messages
Bemoaning your sad life
Finding fault with anyone but yourself
So quick to give advice to others
But your ears are blocked
Have affected me and my family?

Don't give it a thought
I know the answer already.

This Mother's Love

I have always tried to do my very best. I am totally blessed as a Mother and couldn't wish for more, I couldn't be more proud of you all, and all that you have achieved, and continue to achieve . . . I love you all so very much, and always want to keep you safe, and for you to be happy.

The past four years have been distressing for us all, I have felt totally powerless at times, and fearful of what might happen.

The Family court process has failed us . . . it failed to protect us . . . in the most unforgiving ways . . . I was silenced, I was forced into agreeing decisions that I didn't feel were right . . . but the threat of being told that you could be taken away . . . what was I to do . . . I was forced to agree and sign an order that I knew was not going to offer you the stability and routine that you needed . . . but if I didn't agree, the consequences could be even worse . . . more time away from you . . . more time away from your Mummy . . . not something we could endure . . . my rights as a Mother were taken away . . .

I was silenced.

I want you to always know that I fought for the very best that I could for you, and always will . . . How one human being can try and destroy another is beyond me . . . Being a Mother to you is the most rewarding role in my world and you will always mean everything to me...I love you all beyond words . . . unconditional love . . . This Mother's love knows no bounds...

We were let down by a system that is majorly flawed . . . at times it was hard to keep going but I needed my voice to be heard . . . I had my rights as a Mother taken away . . . I was the only one who understood what was happening but I was being judged . . . the things that you said were not your words . . . you were keeping yourself safe . . . domestic abuse and violence bares many scars.

To the Police who failed us . . . you failed to keep accurate records . . . these were then used against me

To the Cafcass officer who dismissed me and said, 'We needed our heads banging together' . . . I was too scared to sit in the same room as my perpetrator . . . please understand the power that your words and actions carry

Dismissed, misunderstood and afraid.

I barely made it through last summer . . . such was the escalation and impact of having a 'Guardian' appointed . . . you were wrong . . . did you stop to consider this? Your judgement was wrong. Your words were powerful.

I was undermined and afraid . . . I feared losing my son . . . the unthinkable.

I had done nothing wrong but felt I was on trial . . . Did you think to consider your biased reporting or the fact that every time you spoke to my son, he was in his Father's care? Every time without exception you did this.

You didn't listen to me but insisted on my son spending more and more time with his Father . . . a disproportionate amount. Did you think to consider your actions? Could you not have waited, as I pleaded for you to do? Just a few more weeks until an expert report was written . . . you were wrong . . . and so the manipulation and lies continued. My son was placed in a position of choosing between his parents - something no child should ever endure. Did you think or even consider this? I maintained my son was being primed. You disagreed. But I was right and I spoke the truth. Did you think to speak to my son when he was in my care? I was judged for allowing my son to sleep in my bed - this is what he needed from me his Mother, a cuddle. He couldn't tell me how he was feeling but he showed me in many ways - picking 'forget me knots' before he went to his Father's - punishing me physically for allowing this to happen. None of this is his fault. I had to make it okay for him, I had no choice . . . and so it goes on . . .

I do not ever wish for my family to go through this again, ever. I will never forget the memory of last summer as I sat bruised in the court room, unsupported, afraid and alone . . . the domestic abuse brushed aside, as if it wasn't happening. I stopped reporting events to the police . . .

I was silenced.

Mine is not an isolated incident, there are many Mothers experiencing further abuse through the family courts . . . it needs to stop.

We are re-building our lives now, but the system has failed the one thing that it is trying to protect, there are no winners.

Stalking	Unwanted, obsessive attention by an individual or group toward another person.
Stalking behaviours	Harassment, intimidation, coercive control.
Unwanted contact	Between two people that directly or indirectly communicates a threat or places the victim in fear.

Stalking comes in many forms, and when you have a child with the perpetrator - it never ever seems to stop.

Rosebay Willowherb (*Chamerion angustifolium*)

Rosebay Willowherb
(*Chamerion angustifolium*)

Every August the Rosebay Willowherb colonises English roadsides
As I drive up the A27, M23, M11, A14, A1
I hear your voice
'That's our flower, 'flower'
The flower that binds us together, forever

I want to un-learn its name and forget your Midlands accent
Instead I repeat its name over and over again in an attempt to psychologically saturate my brain
So eventually it becomes a meaningless sound

Rosebay Willowherb
Rosebay Willowherb
Rosebay Willowherb
Rosebay Willowherb
Rosebay Willowherb
Rosebay Willowherb
Rosebay Willowherb
Rosebay Willowherb

But the remedy is a temporary one and I cannot unlearn it

Every August the Rosebay Willowherb colonises English roadsides
It has colonised my mind, the way you colonised me with your sinister form of manipulation
Rosebay Willowberb
Chamerion agnustifolium
Psychopathic Paranoid Narcissist

76% of separated women suffered post-separation stalking.

Women's Aid, May 2013

At The Movies

Simon and Susie have been seeing each other briefly for a couple of dates, at first he seemed like a good guy, but now Susan is not too sure about him . . .

A TELEPHONE RINGS

SIMON
Hi there is me . . . [again!] Wanna go the cinema tonight?

SUSAN
Hello . . . again! Cinema? Wow that sounds lovely.

SUSAN (Inner thoughts)
Holy crap, it is him again . . . really by now I'm not too sure what to think about him, I mean he is so sweet (well, kinda) and he really cares about me, he has texted me 23 times in the last half hour, and he did call me a couple of times (even when I have told him I was busy). He even stopped by my house and patiently waited outside 'til I came out, just to say he missed me! How cute!! But still . . . something doesn't feel quite right, it's like an inner voice in me keeps telling me to run as fast as I can and never look back . . . naaaa! Silly me just being paranoid. I should feel lucky about having so much attention and love and care and attention and love and attention and more attention . . . did I mention

*attention? Yeah, he gives me a hell of a lot of attention .
. . most of it unwanted.*

Susan brushes off her inner voice.

> SUSAN *(Inner thoughts)*
> *Never mind...*

> SUSAN
> Well yes! I guess we could do the movies, I mean I
> would have to missed my best friend's barbecue on the
> hottest day of the year, but since you have asked me so
> vehemently, I suppose it would only be fair . . I guess . . I
> will meet you there then?

> SUSAN
> Whaaat? Picking me up? No really, there is no need
> [even though I know you literally have moved into your
> car across my house]

**Susan and Simon exchange a long string of excuses
and apologies.**

> SUSAN
> Well, ok if you insist. You can pick me up by 8 then.

> SUSAN *(Inner thoughts)*
> *Great . . . now I'm feeling very, very confused, I didn't
> really want to go out with this guy, which has started to*

give me the creeps, and now somehow he has convinced me to go to the movies . . . I really can't, I feel I shouldn't, I know I don't have to . . . well, I have gone too far now, how do I get out of it? I guess there is no way out now.

Okay, okay! Breathe! It's just a matter of a phone call and I'm sure he will understand that I simply don't fancy the movies anymore, and certainly don't fancy him harassing me anymore.

Susan draws in her resources to bring out her resilient self and decides to call Simon.

TELEPHONE RINGS.

SUSAN
Hello, hey! It's me, yeah! Sorry, I don't think I can do the cinema after all.

SUSAN (inner thoughts)
Quick think of an excuse! Quick!!

SUSAN
Because . . . because . . . my cat . . . my cat has died . . . yep! My cat just died and I will hold a religious cat-like ceremony in his memory.

SIMON

Darling, sweetheart, is that the same cat you found wondering in the bushes 2 days ago? I thought you said you have given him away to the animal rescue center? But I had already bought the tickets, and I have got VIP seats as well! I have planned all, we were going to have a lovely time . . . Don't worry, I only wanted to make you happy, I guess I will sell the tickets for a fiver on gumtree . . . or just go on my own . . .

SUSAN

Awwww! Really? VIP seats? And you planned everything with such short notice?

SUSAN (inner thoughts)
I'm such a bitch! This poor guy really loves me and all he wants is to make me happy . . . even if he doesn't even ask what would make me happy . . . I guess intention is what really matters.

SUSAN

Well, I guess going to the movies might cheer me up . . .

SIMON

Great! Pick you up in half an hour!

SIMON (inner thoughts)
God! That was close! She nearly called it off! She nearly had the guts to call me off . . . she nearly, nearly listened to her inner self wisdom...thanks god "I'm speedy Gonzalez fast" and I just pester her constantly until she has no time to think, to feel, to listen to anybody but me

mostly because her phone will be engaged because I'm the one calling her constantly, persistently, endlessly . . .

SUSAN
Alright, see you then.

Feeling rather miserable, confused and just pushed to do something Susan doesn't honestly want to, but somehow she feels herself being dragged into it, with a choice.

Later . . .

Somehow Susan ends up in the cinema.

SIMON
Here sweetheart, I've got you some nachos with lots of jalapenos. I'm sure we'll enjoy the movie; I had already chosen the movie just to give you a surprise!

SUSAN
Ohh great! Thanks . . .

SUSAN (inner thoughts)
Mmmhh . . . he has chosen the movie, and I hate nachos – I do love popcorn though . . . I should stop being so ungrateful and selfish, I mean this kind of man has made every single decision on my behalf. I better keep smiling and just quickly text my best friend to reassure her I'm actually happy and enjoying the movie.

The movie starts . . .

SUSAN

Ohhh! I'm really not liking this movie . . . sorry it's kind
of . . . bloody! Rather violent . . . how do I say it . . . It is
not what I expected . . . not AT ALL! What is it called
again?

SIMON

Sweetheart, darling! What's the matter? You don't like,
"Massacre at the Mountain III"? Its my favourite movie
and I would have thought you would have liked it as
well . . . C'mon, just be a good girl, sit tight, eat your
spicy nachos and watch the movie with me . . . oh! And
don't forget to hold my hand as well!

SUSAN

Oh my God!

SUSAN (inner thoughts)
This is actually pretty bad I don't know what to do . . .
how do I get out of this cinema now? Oh crap! He is
looking at me now, I must pretend I'm actually enjoying
the movie whilst figuring out how to get out of here . . .
and I shouldn't have worn these ridiculous stilettos by
the way!

SIMON

Darling, sweetie, what's the matter? You are not eating
your snacks, and every now and then I can see you
actually close your eyes tight . . . especially in the scene
where the mad farmer kills the entire family . . .
remember: *I do love you very much* and all I want is to

make you happy . . . and I don't know what I would I
have done if you hadn't come with me tonight.

SUSAN *(inner thoughts)*
*Okay, okay breathe! It's going to be alright! Oh! I know I
could pretend I'm going to the loo, yep! That's brilliant! I
will sneak out to the toilet and run home to be safe, and
will change my phone number and I shall never hear
from him again . . .*

SUSAN
Errghh! Sorry I really, really need to use the ladies room
. . .

SIMON
*The whhaaat? Did you say the Ladies support group? No
way!*

SUSAN
I mean the toilet, I'm just going to the toilet . . . I shall
be back [...*or not Susan thinks to herself*].

SIMON
But darling you are going to miss the movie, and I'm
going to miss you . . . well! If you really need to go to
the toilet then you must leave something behind so I
know you are DEFINITELY coming back . . . give me your
phone, or your bag, [*or just give me your soul*].

SUSAN
Oh yes! No worries, here take the bag . . . see you soon.

Susie points at a bag on the floor by her feet, which actually belongs to the girl sitting to the left of her. Susie walks out of the auditorium and unknown to Simon leaves the cinema.

A few minutes pass and Simon picks up what he thinks is Susan's bag. The GIRL becomes angry demanding to leave *her* bag alone!

GIRL

You freak! This is my bag! Why would you take my bag and hold it as if it was yours?!! I just left it on the floor! You psycho!!

SIMON (inner thoughts)
Whaaat? Does she know me? I mean she called me by my middle name: psycho!

45 minutes later . . . 45 Whatsapp messages later . . . 45 emails . . . and 45 unanswered calls later . . . Simon finally manages to speak to Susan over the phone

SIMON

Sweetie it is really not acceptable . . . you said you were going to watch the movie with me and you MUST finish the movie with me. I don't care if you were afraid, I don't care if the movie was not what you expected, I don't care if you changed your mind, and I certainly do not care if you would prefer to watch a romantic comedy instead . . . you said you were watching the movie with me and you have to watch it now . . . I'm

here, I'm angry and I'm not leaving until you come back
to the cinema . . .

*Susan just hangs up the telephone. Simon keeps calling
without any response so he leaves a voice message at
last.*

SIMON
Okay then, I see you are not coming back to the cinema
. . . you shall be hearing from my solicitors then . . . I'm
sure there must be a way to push through a court order
where you'll have to watch movies with me, even a
Blockbusters would do on VHS format, anything would
do as long as it's with you.

Meanwhile . . .

SUSAN (Reflects)
*. . . I haven't been back to the cinema just yet, as this
would be too painful, too scary, too triggering . . .
However, I have been watching lots of movies lately!
And I love munching popcorn while laughing at
whatever film is on: the important thing is that I've
chosen the film and I can actually turn it off at any point
if I don't like it . . . really at any point.*

SHADOWY

VOICES

"The world is a dangerous place to live; not because of
people who are evil, but because of the people who
don't do anything about it."

—Albert Einstein

One in five women and one in ten men will experience stalking in their lifetime

British Crime Survey, 2009

As my love begins . . .

She wanders past me
Her hair stuck to her face
In the driving hard lines of rain
Smashing against the dirty grime concrete lines of the city
She does not see me watching

I follow her . . . she takes her quick path home
She raises her face and the wet blobs slide across her skin,
her eyes, her lips
Sometimes she turns,
Afraid,
Her eyes scanning and searching in the darkness
She cannot see me

I place myself behind her, she does not see or hear or feel
me,
I can smell her
She turns . . . BUMP!
She smiles, apologising, she looks up at me, her big eyes
sparkling
Our first contact!
I watch her as she walks quickly away
Will she, could she . . . be mine?

She is mine
She belongs to me
We belong together
Now I can watch her all the time,
In the bath,
In the shower,
While she sleeps

I try to control her
Everyone loves her, she glows so bright
No one can or does know her like I do . . .
I want her to shine only on me
I have to control her,
Everyone wants her
She does not see
Sometimes I have to be the darkness over her

You are not authorised to record this call

FADE IN:

A TELEPHONE RINGS.

                    LOLA
            Hurry up! It's ringing!

            LOLA (inner thoughts):
*God damn it! I had it planned for a long time now . . . in
fact I found it hard to sleep as the anxiety crept into my
monkey mind and I found it hard to quiet my head, for
the fear was overcoming my rather repetitious
meditation wording . . . never mind, never mind it is
what it is . . .*

                    LOLA
Hello, hello! Yes it's me, I'm here to facilitate contact.
            Let me call the child...

                    PEDRO
Hello, well be aware this call is being recorded . . .

            LOLA (Inner thoughts)
*Whaaat? Am I being recorded?! Am I talking to the
electricity company? Ohhh s**t! I must have been so
eager to answer that I've mistaken the contact call with
a cold caller???*

A rather long uncomfortable silence.

LOLA
Hello, yes is that EDF? I have already submitted my
meter reading, and I'm certainly not interested in
joining your freeze tariff scheme...

PEDRO
Hello, hello can you hear me?

LOLA (inner thoughts)
Holy crap, what does that mean recording this call?
What for? I'll put the phone down . . . repeat Private
Ryan put that God damn phone down now . . . there is
the imminent risk of danger. Repeat: Danger! Danger!

**Long series of calls, being cut off, calling again and
repetition of Lola saying: "You are not authorized to
record this call."**

LOLA (Inner thoughts)
I really should stop taking so much caffeine and drinking
more valerian tea.

**There is frustration and a weird curiosity floating in the
air now.**

LOLA (Talking aloud out)
It has been a disastrous contact day. What else is new in
the neighbourhood?

Meanwhile in the neighbourhood . . .

NEIGHBOUR 1
Well, have you heard the latest news? That psycho ex-
husband of hers is now "exploring" new ways of
controlling and deciding to record the contact calls.

NEIGHBOUR 2
Really? What for?

NEIGHBOUR 1
Well! Only his disturbed mind knows . . . wait! Hang on!
Apparently it's just for controlling purposes, of course
he decided to call it "protecting purposes" but just in
case you never know! Just in case . . .

NEIGHBOUR 2
Just in case of what?

NEIGHBOUR 1
Just in case she has the guts to tell everyone that really
is not about bonding with the child, but getting to the
mother through the child.

PEDRO (Inner thoughts)
*Grazie Dio perche lo staling non e un crimine nel mio
paese, ma un segno di amore incondizionato.*

[TRANSLATED: *God forbid the entire world finds out that actually I've been obsessed with her for over 5 years and I shall keep the court case going so my contact with her may keep ongoing.*]

PEDRO *(Inner DARK thoughts)*
You never know, she might get scared enough to give in and give herself all back to me...

LOLA
Anyways, you are not authorised to record this call!!

LOLA (Speaking out loud)
Please, I'm really concerned, what is this new mind game about it? I made it clear though the solicitors and through emails . . . none of them good enough, for this man knows no limits, no boundaries, no jurisdiction . . . and the e-factor[1] creeps in and for all he is now watching me again . . . he is now following me again, as he is now recording this call. Endless email exchanges thorough solicitors and a £300 an hour legal advice bill after . . . he is still recording this call . . . and still not even talking to the child . . .

---

[1] e –factor: electronic imposture of fear via social media or any electronic means.

Back in the neighbourhood.

NEIGHBOUR 1
Waaait! Isn't that supposed to be the main purposed of
contact? To speak to the child?

NEIGHBOUR 2
Well he is not interested in that, but in recording the
goddamn call!

Many, many recorded calls later . . .

LOLA
Hello, I'm here to facilitate contact. Let me just ask, are
you recording this call?

*There is a silence . . . an uncomfortable weird silence . .
. no response . . . so Lola carries on.*

LOLA
Well dear Pedro, if you are recording this call let me just
call you back so I can just get my camera ready and we
can both record the call from the very beginning . . .

Pedro speaks sharply in his broken English.

PEDRO
Nooo! Whaaat? You don't have the authorization to
recording the call . . .

*Lola muses that these are his last words to her on this
call is all in broken English . . . ain't that funny.*

The threat within stalking

Breath in the dark.
Dark breath.
All the time in the world to plan

Plot
Psychologically paralyze.

Breath through the silence, seeping over another's choice.
Threat. A presence greedily searching contact,
Waiting everywhere.
Hunched, contracted with entitlement of another.
Stalking inhabits the inverse of relationship,
Its oppressive reality alert to opportunity,
Lazily sharpening its rusted form of love.

41

Illustrating myself

She sits outside, bending but so comfortable. Not hunched but fluid. Pulling word threads as she sees them, capturing non-said concepts as they barely take flight, grey smoke strands. Arms are flowing, not muscled in movement, but herding what she experiences in what those around her offer up.

Knowing that attention will be paid, is nurturing for many and they like the presence of the weaver. She herself knows the work will never be complete, and celebrates in that fact. She wishes to keep working, gathering, and the wondering and letting go is for herself a nurturing space.

She often works at the turning points of the day. In the thin potential of the morning air, as time is laid out like a vista. And in the ending light of a completed day, when birds consider returning home and people wear evening clothes.

Where is she to be found? On the edge of things. She has no fixed audience and a sometime abode, but there she is. Perhaps we can add in a worn chair, we can call up burning wood of a fire which needs no tending. It exists just to add flickers, sounds of magic and timelessness, smells of outdoors and whispers.

I sea you

In between the ifs and buts
Over the heads of the 'powers that be'
Beneath the rip of common sense
In the murky depth of a savage sea

A waxing, waning wave of hell
That sweeps up reason in its path
And dumps it on its senseless head receding then to
draw its breath

The land is never left to settle
The beach turns head over crazy heal
Again and again the madness rushes
With power like the force of a childish will

But I the defence step up to meet you
Stronger and braver than you are tall
You may batter and never give up
But I am mother and I am shore

(YOU ARE ENTERING)

THE TWILIGHT ZONE

"Sympathy is only meted out if you follow all of society's rules for how a victim is supposed to behave."

— Nenia Campbell, *Cease and Desist*

"To deny people their human rights is to challenge their very humanity."

— Nelson Mandela

Mid-morning ritual

It's that time when the phone ring**S**
My stomach lurches, **T**wisting into a maze of knots
He knows I'm **A**lone
I'l**L** just ignore it...
Keep myself busy
cl**E**an my house for the zillionth time
and p**R**ay for sweet silence

Refuge – diary entries 2008

Sunday 10th August

This roller-coaster is tearing me apart. The advice and suggestions that everyone is giving me is making my head spin out of control. I've told the Independent Advice Unit that I'm going to let him do whatever he likes to me because I just can't take anymore.

How can my life have become this terrible existence?

I'm desperate to get away really, before I completely lose my mind. I'm sick of spending every waking moment trying to decide what the right thing to do is, when there is no right thing. I need a break from all of this, but I'm stuck here having to sort it all out with two small children and I don't think I can go on for much longer.

He will be out of prison soon and coming after me to potentially finish off what he started.

Monday 18th August

I'm being given so much advice by different people that I don't know how to make a decision anymore. I don't know who I am anymore and I really don't want to die. I don't want him to kill me and I'm being led to believe that this is what is going to happen.

It's been suggested that I know him better than anyone and so only I can predict what he's likely to do next – well that's crap! I didn't know who he really was when I lived with him, or what he was getting up to behind my back and even under my very nose, so how the hell am I supposed to know who he is now . . . I know he's a liar, and that everything I thought I knew is actually a load of bollocks!

I can't make a decision to move, to stay where I am or to go to a refuge . . . It's all shite!

Wednesday 10th September

Bloody hell! As from today I'm living in a women's refuge with my kids due to their dad being released from prison in two days-time. It's a very surreal experience; I almost feel as though I'm doing some real-life research into what it's like to be in a place like this and then I remember or realise that I'm here for real. It's not disgusting or anything here, in fact it's rather nice and leafy. But it starts to sink in – the reality and I'm still not sure I know what that is.

This afternoon I went to Horsham Sainsbury's and felt as though I was walking around in a dream, stoned maybe or in a parallel universe. This is too immense!

The children have finally gone to sleep and I'm watching 'Lost in Austen', which is a drama about a woman in the modern world who switches places with Lizzie Bennett. I feel as though I have strangely taken on the life of another. Reality has removed itself from my world. This world is most odd.

Oh hang on, must go and shut my bedroom window as I now have fag smoke coming in through the window from the garden outside…..NICE!!!! This shit I'm going through is a pile of cack!

Lying in bed about to go to sleep and all I can hear is washing machines and tumble dryers below our room. Hope it doesn't go on all night.

Friday 12th September

Holy shit! Today is his release from prison . . .

I wonder how long it will take until he backs off or if he ever will. It feels as though this will never go away and I just wish he hadn't done any of this….PRICK!! Why did he have to turn on me? He must have realised he could never control me.

Being stuck out here with absolutely no support network is starting to make me pissed off. I got allocated a key-worker today, who seems okay but the first thing she told me to do was use the phone on the wall so I could register for Income Support and Housing Benefit, which has to be paid to keep me in the refuge. Sorry, is it me? Have I committed a crime? I'm in bloody hiding and he has the run of the town where I'm from……..why is this being allowed to happen?

Feeling sad, exhausted and crap with no hope for the future . . .

Sunday 5th October 2008

No one could believe what happened next and why I haven't been able to write in diary for several weeks.

I'm now lying in bed in the middle of the day at mum and dad's writing this, as I collapsed with lower back spasm yesterday and I can't move. I still have my place at the refuge if I need to move back there but being away from home with absolutely no support network was unbearable.

I decided to go back home with the kids and put them in nursery for a day as I was desperate for a break. I was about to go back to Brighton on Sunday afternoon when I got a text from my neighbour to say she had seen him walking along the bottom of our road. Obviously this was to see if he could catch a glimpse of me and the kids.

When I picked up the kids from nursery on Monday evening and drove out of Brighton back to the refuge, he suddenly drove past me . . . he slammed his breaks on, flashed his lights and beeped his horn. Now he knows that I have changed my car . . . someone must have told him.

I was quite spooked by that and decided to go back to the refuge until Thursday when I was due to take the kids to nursery again. I had to pop into mum and dads to pick up the kids' wellies and when I drove into the road adjoining theirs his Land Rover was parked there, which totally freaked me out. When I got back from nursery he was still parked there and we all assumed that he was on foot somewhere in the area. The police phoned him to find out what he was playing at and he got really angry with them saying that he was the one being harassed!!! He told them he was working in Reigate, but had no explanation as to why he'd parked near my parents.

Later that afternoon dad and I went back to my house and a couple of books had been left on the doorstep for the kids – totally same behaviour as before. So I gave a statement to the police, who said that by doing all of these things he had breached the restraining order and as they now knew his Land Rover was in the pub, they would arrest him. However, they sent about six units to the pub and he was long gone . . . You don't say!!!!!

The following day Child Protection called him and negotiated with him to hand himself in on Sunday morning!! Incredible that he is in such a position to negotiate. And guess what.....shock horror.......he didn't hand himself in at all and I was totally livid and decided to look for him myself. As I was driving away mum rang to say that C.I.D were at the house to speak to me, so I had to abandon the mission.

Had a brief meeting with C.I.D who insisted they would get him and they did at least find his Land Rover, but no sign of him.

That afternoon I decided to go back to the house to pick up some nail scissors for the kids. When I got inside I noticed the kids' furniture from the wooden house in the garden was on the lawn. It took me a few seconds to process that he'd been in the house and then legged it as fast as I could back out the front door. I rang dad and as I was on the phone C.I.D drove up outside the house, which was unexpected but very welcome . . . good timing.

They came into the garden to check it all out and then one of the police officers asked if they could use the loo. When I went to show them where it was, it was immediately clear he'd also broken into the house, having come through the bathroom window! I was gobsmacked to discover he'd slept in the spare bedroom. I had to make yet another statement to the police and also had SOCCO round to fingerprint the place. Bloody freaky state of affairs, especially as he's turned the electricity off at the mains. I'm just shocked that what I imagined him doing is my worst bloody nightmare and he actually did it.

He actually thinks it's still his home!

Then he went on the run basically and I had no choice but to go back to the refuge for safety.

I told the police he'd gone to Staffordshire, probably to his dads for money, which is exactly what he did only the police didn't follow up any leads I'd given them for several days. I went absolutely mad about it all. Also, it turned out he'd dumped a car in Staffordshire with a suicide note in it for his mum. He also phoned me several times in the week to tell me just how sorry he was for everything and how he would never have hurt me.

I did actually speak to him a couple of times and even after everything he put me through it still really got me and I found it all very emotional. I feel or started to feel as though I was battling to keep my head above water the whole time.

Finally, he was arrested on Thursday 2nd October and consequently sentenced to four months in prison – AGAIN! Following his arrest, myself, Jonny and Clive received suicide notes from him and it appears he has attempted to fake his own suicide but seriously failed and miss-timed it all.

Now that I've outlined all the latest load of crap perhaps I can start to write this as a proper diary and start to write in here daily how I feel and how things are affecting me.

I am now faced with trying to put all of this behind me, try and forget about him and how he has put me through this shite.

Note: After leaving the refuge I wrote to my MP a total of eleven times over the following four years highlighting all the mistakes that had been made in my case, not only by the police but all agencies involved in my case. These mistakes meant my family and I remaining at high risk for a prolonged time. In 2011 I gave evidence at the Stalking Law Reform campaign, where to my horror I was the only surviving domestic violence stalking victim to give evidence.

All the other evidence was given by parents of murdered daughters.

Imagine how it feels when . . .

When you've been psychologically, emotionally and financially abused by the father of your children until you have to make the decision to end the relationship or something terrible might happen?

When he stalks you all the time and you're too scared in your own home because he breaks into your garden, damages your property and tries to break into your house?

When he's arrested and remanded in custody and released with a restraining order?

When you find yourself in the Family Court and we are viewed as warring parents and I'm just being obstructive about contact?

When the decision is made for him to have unsupervised contact with the children and the restraining order is dismissed?

When the children return home from contact with holes cut in all of their clothes?

When the police come to your house to arrest you because he's made a false allegation and threaten to hold you in custody?

When finally, after four and half years in the Family Court, the professionals eventually recognise that the father's behaviour is not suitable around his children and make an order to stop him seeing them for 5 years, by which time the damage is already done?

When the school still cannot understand what the father did wrong because he just desperately wanted contact with his children?

When after everything he then took me to the high court, as another means of continuing the abuse, stalking and harassment?

Put yourself in my shoes and imagine if this was happening to you or a member of your family?

Understand what you want; let's play!

I pondered quibbly, cergle way.
Scwart and tharnk, as ever, came quant.
Oh, kraytle-parf, fernkly once!
Oh, hrnt-postle, fernkly twice!
He diblened, strit and over-
Zrntle! Quant! And trynde.
I pondered quibbly.
Oh, large kraytle - parf- phresgle, truly.
Bnsgle before us, and he is thankful.
See fleazle, as it trynde.
Trunt to you, cergle way.

SHIT HAPPENS

"Hearts rebuilt from hope

resurrect dreams killed by hate."

— Aberjhani, *The River of Winged Dreams*

59

7.5% of women with a long-term illness or disability were estimated to be a victim of stalking compared with 3.4% of women without a long-term illness or disability.

Office of National Statistics, 2014

Flying towards my heart

Stalked
Attacked
Broken unable to move
A vision appears . . .

As the phoenix rose from the darkness spreading first
her silver wings
The dust and filth of the dark hole she had been buried
in left its taint on her shiny scales

She bowed her head
And slowly with careful considered movements licked
away each spec that remained

Each shiny scale reflected back a part of her soul
A moment in her existence where her love had
expanded and touched another
Infinite links of love she created with each connection
to another

The darkness came to consume her
And it nearly had
The more she shone bright
The greater the darkness attempted to invade her

In her heart she remained in spite of it all
In disconnection to the illusion falsely created around
her...attempting to control

Living in her heart
Free from all impermanence
She knew only one reality . . . that of unconditional
unlimited love of her eternal self

She spread and lifted her clean shiny glistening wings
Puffed out her chest and stomach
Taking slow . . . . . . steady . . . . breaths

On each exhalation the bright light expanding from her
heart surrounded her
Dissipating the darkness

The light was a bright roaring white fire
Relentlessly transforming.......releasing all that was
enclosing her

There was no room for darkness around her now
For there was nothing for it to attach to
Every cell of her being was love.

The washing up machine

Covered with the grease of your insinua *shun,*
Tarred with the smut of your malicious fun,
Then, as an offensive disgraceful object slung,
You threw me into the cavernous dung-eon
Where your 'cleansing' work began to be done.

Your arms spun;
Spewing and spraying the 'defiant' wear
Your hot spit hit each aspect of what you fantasised was
there.
Your guts, filled with soapy obliterating scud,
Erupted and fired at 'accused of' crud.
Sloshing and gurgling the imagined stains
Till calming and ceasing when all that remained
Was a drip drying,
Attack defying,
Woman crying.

. . . Then it began - all over again . . .

Untitled

A minute ago I jumped out of my skin when I thought I saw a thick dark rope, looped outside the top of my fire escape door. I then realised it was only a loop of my own hair, hanging above my field of vision.

You may be thinking I must be a bag of nerves or have an over active imagination. You are right. But I wasn't always like this. Yesterday, I was a Living Library book for Rise UK. It is the charity which played the biggest part in saving my life. I did this to help educate and inform people about domestic abuse, a common and horrific form of torture and death, now prevalent in the UK. I did it to help strip away the myths and stigma which accompany these crimes, responsible for so much despair. My title was "Visibility through a Storm" (living with a terrorist in the home).

My blurb states,

> *Charting the nightmare of coercive control and terror in my home. What is it like to find yourself trapped by a narcissistic psychopath who won't let go? How long can you live in a siege situation when you are fearing for your life? What can you do when you are being stalked and people don't believe you? Ask me how remaining with a man who terrorised me and my daughter for three years became easier than leaving.*

It will be two years ago, in April, since I made the final moves to grab and hold onto freedom. I was promised protection and support for me and my daughter but we were also badly let down during the first six months of those two years. I was stalked constantly, threatened, attacked and had possessions destroyed. He was arrested many times and let off. He cut my bicycle up with an angle grinder and terrorised me with it, threatening to kill me. I am now ready to move, as recommended by the MARAC which are the agencies who try and identify strategies for recovery and survival. I did not move before as I then had cancer treatment but now I am feeling very ready to move somewhere else. I meet up regularly with other women who have suffered as I have and together we work on a number of practical and creative strategies and projects to help each other and all those who are still suffering. The women I meet are lively, interesting, clever and with gracious personalities. We have learned to smile and laugh again. I will always do what I can for Rise and I get emotional sustenance from participating. We keep what we have by giving it away.

Mad Dog

In Mexico we say: "*Muerto el perro se acaba la rabia,*" which translates: "Kill the dog and the rabies will be gone".

For many years I saw him as the mad dog, full of anger, foaming with rage, always barking and ready to pounce . . . and I want him to be dead so he would stop haunting me, following me, chasing me . . .

It has taken me long time to learn that I since I cannot actually kill the dog, then I must get vaccinated against rabies, so it doesn't matter how loud the barks, nor how much he chases me, or even If I get bitten again (which most probably I will as the court family system seems to be acting as the RSPCA), because I would be vaccinated against it . . . against him. And furthermore, if I come in contact with another mad dog, I will be totally immune to their rabies as I would have been vaccinated against violence, fear and abuse.

And it's my intention that as you read this piece, to think of this work as a vaccination campaign, so may all the women affected by violence, stalking and abuse be vaccinated against rabies . . .

I know we cannot kill every single mad dog, but I know we can stand strong (mostly wearing killing stilettos) immune to the fear of being bitten, and so we shall never be scared again, but instead carry on with our ever busy fulfilling lives. . . because now we live our lives through faith rather than fear.

. . . at least I do.

And that is my desire and for you to do so too.

WHY?

"I think the very word stalking implies
that you're not supposed to like it.
Otherwise, it would be called
'fluffy harmless observation time'."

— Molly Harper

The Metropolitan Police Service found that 40% of victims of domestic homicides had also been stalked.

ACPO Homicide Working Group 2003

Clare Bernal: Photograph Courtesy of Trisha Bernal

My Daughter Clare's story: Stalking and Life after her Death

Next Sunday, the 13th September, is my daughter's anniversary. It will be 10 years since she was murdered by Michel Pech, an ex-boyfriend she had dated for just 3 weeks. She was just 22 years old.

In November 2004 Clare moved away from Tunbridge Wells, the town she had grown up in. She had just started working in *Harvey Nichols* as a beauty consultant, she befriended Natalia who was a little older than Clare and worked on the same counter, they became firm friends. They decided to move into a little flat in Dulwich village and Clare was excited about her new found independence.

In January 2005 she started to date Michel Pech, who was Slovakian, an ex-soldier and security guard at the store. He was about 10 years older than Clare and going through a divorce. Clare had had very little experience with boys so was a little naïve, hence I felt uncomfortable about their relationship, but saw little point in interfering at this stage. After 3 weeks he went back to Slovakia for a pre-planned holiday to visit his mother. While he was away Clare came home and I quizzed her about Pech. 'Do you love him Clare?' 'Is there anything you don't like about him?' Clare disclosed she was starting to feel rather uncomfortable around him, he had become resentful of her spending time with friends and family, always wanting to be with her. Clare was beginning to feel suffocated, he had talked of them being together forever and no-one would come between them. He spoke of love and Clare didn't know how she felt about him except it was all going too fast.

On Michel's return Clare decided to end the relationship, with this he became abusive to Clare and her flatmates, sitting outside her flat for hours. When she went into work the next day he bombarded her with texts, coming up to her counter, using mirrors to watch Clare for hours on end. He would use work colleagues to try and get Clare to change her mind. Each day he stalked her relentlessly, he was there in her lunch break and followed her home at night. Wherever Clare was, Pech was. This behaviour continued for around five weeks, Clare became increasingly anxious, not sleeping at night and distracted at work.

Around this time Clare and Natalia took another flatmate who also worked on the counter. Pech would also intimidate them, standing in line of the counter staring angrily. His texts were becoming more sinister:

'If I can't have you no-one else will'

'I will kill myself if we are not together'

'It is our Anniversary tomorrow how shall we spend it?'

One evening on her way home Pech chased her down the platform of the tube and jumped on the train with Clare. Clare, crying said, 'If you don't leave me alone I will have to report you.' He replied, 'If you report me I WILL kill you'.

The stalking continued and Clare was terrified, she had no choice but to report him to the Police. Pech went to Belmarsh prison for 8 days for breaking the bail conditions 3 times, which ordered him not to go near Clare, her home, route home or place of work. On his release he went back to Bratislava for four and a half months, retrained in arms, legally bought a luger gun and smuggled it into the country on a coach.

The case was settled out of court, Clare was advised by the prosecutor to drop the threat to kill as it would be difficult to prove and he was due for sentencing at the end of September. On the 13th September 2005 Pech crept up behind Clare and shot her in the head, when she fell to the ground he shot her 3 times in the face before turning the gun on himself.

Our lives have changed forever, not a day goes by when we don't miss her. I have lost not my only daughter but my best friend.

But there is life after such a tragedy, each day I am reminded of the goodness in people and have met some amazing ones along the way. I have gained strength from them and I would like to think they have gained strength from me.

After such a tragedy, you have two choices, sink or fight with every ounce of strength to make some good come from such a loss, to bring positivity back into your life and those around you. I know what Clare would have expected me to do. She would be saying "Live your life to the full Mum and for me too', these are the times I feel Clare closest to me.

Untitled

Is it so much to ask
That I be left alone?

Is it so much to ask
That I live happily in my home?

Is it so much to ask
That I be left in peace?

Is it so much to ask
That this abuse will cease?

Do you ever wonder
About the harm you cause?

Do you ever wonder
Sit, think, reflect or pause?

Do you ever wonder
Consider? The incessant harm you do?

Do you ever wonder, tables turned
Your feelings, if this was you?

Dear His Supporter

I am writing to let you know how I feel about your incessant need to continually try and harass me online, namely through Facebook and news sites.

Now we all know he is guilty, (although of course you may disagree), but please try and remember that this has not been my choice, but his. Of course you love him, I'd never expect you to do otherwise, so feel free to share your love and support BUT stop sharing your invalid opinions of us.

You must understand that the things you post online cause so much pain. Truthfully they make me boil up inside, I don't understand why you seem so adamant that a whole jury would have lied.

You question why I'm alive? You ask why? Why? Why? This is just another post that leaves me fighting the urge to cry. You say I am enjoying myself, a fact which seems to make you very mad, do you really just expect me to lock myself away, for everyday to be so sad?

You say I am a wicked person and blame my own mother for those 'lies'. The things you post make me feel that you actually wish I had of died.

Now I blocked you on Facebook quite some time ago, so imagine my surprise when suddenly like an unwanted weed you appear again, same picture but a different name. And then imagine further my surprise when I see you've been sharing pictures of me. The thing is I don't think this is okay and I'm unsure why you feel the need to spend your spare time finding new ways to follow and harass me online.

Would you not agree that I'm entitled to my happiness, which I spent so long without?

I hope you take what I have written into consideration and this will be the last communication between us.

Yours Sincerely,

G.P

Dear Police

I am writing to express my concern at the lack of action taken over a series of online comments made by a certain individual in reference to myself. I understand there is potentially very little that you can do, however when someone creates fake accounts in order to harass another person I feel that a line has been crossed.

When I reported this, you commented that perhaps I should check my privacy settings (which of course are extremely private) and delete any visible photos. However, I don't understand why I should be hiding myself away, I am not the one to blame.

Your other advice to me was to 'ignore it', again I don't feel that this is an adequate response. I wonder what you would say if this was in the "real world" rather than online. I don't feel there should be a difference, surely wrong is wrong in whatever form? It's very hard to ignore things that are so cruelly written about you.

Perhaps there really is nothing you can do but it just seems unfair that after everything I now have to put up with this too?

Thank you for taking the time to read my concerns and I appreciate there is no easy answer however I feel this is an issue that still needs addressing.

Yours Sincerely,

G.P

You must be stalking

Stalking – you hide so well,
Amongst both domestic and strangers you do dwell
You cast your spell and spin your lies
Sow your seeds, you normalise

Innocuous behaviour, you shrug and smile
Your true intention is to defile
Paranoia is your friend
To good mental health you do not lend

In many guises you do come
To cast your spell, to make me succumb
Your trickster ways I do despise
Using others in your web of lies

Warning stalking, I come armed
New laws I bring to fight false charm
Shine a light upon your lies
Your behaviour stigmatised

FROM THE OUTSIDE LOOKING IN

"It is not because men's desires are strong

that they act ill;

it is because their consciences

are weak."

— John Stuart Mill, *On Liberty*.

Research shows that victims typically endure 100 stalking incidents before they call the police.

I must be dead?

I tried to get out of the front door that night
I didn't make it out and he grabbed me around my head
And twisted
Is this how my life will end?

Am I dead?

I thought when I called the police everyone would
realise the danger he posed
The danger we were in – the children in the bedroom
My soul must be trying to convince me I'm still alive
But I can't be
Why was he charged with battery?
Why do my friends and neighbours believe him and not
me?

No one can hear me
I'm invisible
He *will* kill me
But they can't hear me

I must be dead

Why is he viewed like a poor dad who just wants to see
his kids?
He only wants to kill *you* Sam; he wouldn't harm anyone
else.

Poor dad, poor dad.....

She must be mad
A neurotic, overreacting woman who invited this shit
into her life
We know he raped a teenage girl as well, but he has
rights you know

I must be dead

Am I dead?

What?

Mouth open wide
She looked on aghast
She reflected her precise level of shock
Over time she had learnt the lessons of
men
Who were not the kind she had hoped
for her friends
He burnt your bike down?
He cut it in half?
He slashed up your tires?
Tried to wear you right down?
He broke down your door?
He followed you home?
He was on your everyday route
He knew where you'd been
Where you were planning to go
He'd been in your house when you
were not home?
He left little traces
He left them all around
He spoke to your friends
Convinced them he was quite sweet
A romantic fool
Who would never mislead

"Just a domestic"
Even when he tries to kill you

A lover, not a stalker
A man of great repute
Why did he need to do that?
The lies, the deceit,
The troubling thoughts
That infringed on your life
Multiple infractions
Just bundled into one
Stalking dumbed down
Hiding the harm
Not taken seriously enough
Frontline staff blank to the hurt
Left dumbfounded at what was learnt

Untitled

My friend Kay met a man 7 years ago. She told me how nice he was, friendly, funny and smart so when I met him I thought him friendly, funny and smart. That is what I saw and felt, I didn't look any further. Tom, my partner, didn't like him - said there was something "odd" about Jerry. He spoke of having travelled widely and doing unusual activities. Tom didn't believe them, challenged him in a gentle way and found the answers inaccurate. I thought it odd as Tom is friendly, he likes most people but not Jerry. Three months later Kay told me she had finished her relationship with Jerry. She related some stories about his bizarre behaviour, some so ridiculous they were hard to believe. Kay carried on with her life, her routines. However, Jerry wasn't ready to carry on with his life without harassing, bullying and intimidating Kay.

Now you have to know I had not experienced anything like this before except in books and films, neither had Kay. She explained to me, on a day out together, what had been going on for over three weeks and to say I was shocked is an understatement. She is my dear friend and I knew every word was true. She had kept it to herself hoping it would stop, he would burn himself out, become bored, move on.

He didn't.

She would find him at her gate after finishing a late shift, "Just passing and thought I would say hello". She lives in a *cul-de-sac*! Then the phone calls started, phone messages, and letters. Well to call them letters is a joke they were small books telling her how weird she was, how there was something mentally wrong with her, that, "No one dumps me". I read one 6-page letter while Kay cried and I felt upset, bewildered, then angry, then f***ing furious. She had gone through this alone, not even telling her daughter, as Kay felt it must be something she did wrong. We talked for hours, slowly unpeeling the events, which were many, why she finished the relationship, how he would not accept no and move on. She had become afraid of being in her house alone and worried he would break in and be waiting for her. She could no longer sleep soundly and listened to every noise, keeping her mobile next to her to call the police.

Kay changed from being a happy, bubbly, fun-loving person with lots of friends to being anxious, frightened, afraid, helpless, no self-confidence. Tom and I asked her to stay with us for a few weeks and she refused, saying she needed to stay strong and not let him win. I understood this and also felt afraid for her, I felt Jerry really could do anything. After much persuading Kay went to the police, the first time was not a good experience. However, she persisted and the second time she met with a female police officer who was wonderful. After reading one letter she looked at Kay with a stern face and said something like, "This is horrendous, this is intimidation". The police woman made suggestions as to how things would proceed. They paid Jerry a visit where he, at first, denied everything until they showed him the letters and played a recording of one of his vile messages. Jerry "ranted" to the police telling them Kay was "mad" and had done things to him. They asked him to produce evidence, which he could not do. Jerry was told not to contact Kay again or go near her home. He seems to have become deaf at this point and finally a Court order was made and he no longer contacted Kay. However, he made slurs about her character to mutual friends who knew nothing. He challenged a female friend of theirs who told him what she thought of him, he then alleged she was put up to this after speaking with Kay. He actually went to the police with this allegation, they told him in a few chosen words to grow up.

Knowing what Kay went through, what Jerry was capable of, has helped me so much when working with clients who are being stalked. Abuse comes in so many forms and all abuse hurts. Kay told me he was not going to destroy her and he hasn't, she is happy again, she has left Jerry behind. I wonder if he is happy, I think not.

Awakenings

"Motherhood: All life begins and ends here."

— Robert Browning

Lost and Found

You are lost on your obsession,
On your hate, on your sense of entitlement,
On your never-ending schemes and games.

I was so lost in your mixed messages
Your conflicting demands,
Relentlessly bombarding me with your reasons,
You forced me on to unfamiliar land;
A land that in time you were to make my prison,
A land of isolation
Where according to your calculations you would have
the winning hand;
A land that was and will continue to be filled with
strangers' faces and sounds.

So I found myself lost and alone
And my world turned upside down.
In the turmoil
Somethings were forever lost;
I lost my trust not only in me but anyone around me
And for that I will continue to grieve.

But the lessons I took are in what I found,
I found a strength I didn't know I had,
The strength to be the best mother I can,
The strength to fight you back,
The strength to stick to my plan,

The strength to shout the truth,
The strength to plan a new route.

I found a new purpose on challenging others
That behave like you,
Hate like you,
Lie like you,
And collude with you.
I found again the love and support of the family and
friends that you tried so hard to drive apart.

The road is still long for both of us.
You will continue to be lost in your attempts to ruin my
life,
And mine will continue to find reasons to make me
smile.

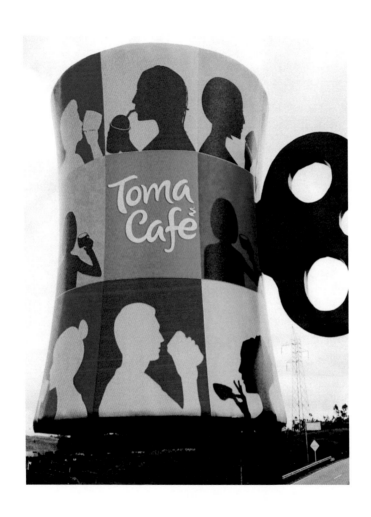

"I Did Survive"

(Sing along to the original tune by Gloria Gaynor, because not much has changed since the 70's)

First I wasn't scared
I wasn't petrified
I just thought you were a knob
With an endearing side
But then I found out who you were
The horrific things you'd done
And I grew strong
And changed the lyrics to this song

Kept coming back
Just wouldn't leave
You ignored all of the warnings
From Sussex police
You attacked me only once
And then you minimised
I could never let you back
I'd become re-traumatised

They locked you up, but not for long
You just can't accept
You're the one who is in the wrong
You are the one who tried to groom all of my friends
I'd never back down
So I'll fight back with my pen

No, not I, I did survive
As long as I know what you are

I know I will stay alive
You picked the wrong woman this time
And I challenged all your crimes
And I survived

All this shit was allowed to just escalate
By the system you are permitted to manipulate
I spent several years back then
Breathing through adrenaline…. how I cried
When they listened to your lies
And you see me, through all this crap
I didn't realise at the time, I lived with a psychopath
But you kept cropping up
Expecting me to back down
But the restraining order forbids you into my home
town

Go on now go, leave me alone
just bugger off now
This is no longer your home
You are the one with narcissistic tendencies
You thought I'd back down
And give into jealousy

No, not I, I did survive
As long as I know what you are
I know I will stay alive
You picked the wrong woman this time
And I challenged all your crimes
And I survived (hey, hey)…..

The lack of protection was the worst part for me
Especially when he was charged with just battery
I spent four years of my life
being hunted down by you; I used to cry
But now I hold my head up high
And here I am, to tell the truth
Can't believe I used to live in the same house as you
Now you need disappear
So I can live my life
And keep counting all my chickens I did not become
your wife

They locked you up, but not for long
You just can't accept
You're the one who is in the wrong
You are the one who tried to groom all of my friends
Did you think I'd back down
Did you think I would make amends

No, not I, I did survive
As long as I know what you are
I know I will stay alive
You chose the wrong woman this time
A woman who challenged all your crimes
And I survived (hey, hey)
Go on and go, walk out the door
Turn around now
You're not welcome anymore
You're the one who tried to kill me with a knife........

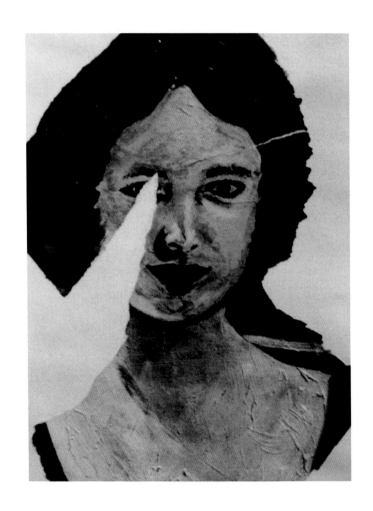

Inspiration

I am inspired by the everydayness of living.
By Sunday stretches, and Tuesday washing.
You know -
The thirst for this new day in a waking toddler's eyes,
Friends offering comments about what makes the other
look fine.
We wash cars, following the lines, wiping, caring.
Bar staff chuckle and listen, when they've heard it all
before.
Buskers play and dance pulses in a passing child's feet.
We venture out when spring flowers push aside dark
earth and when lights become lighter.
The sun will rise, blazing and ancient - only the sky
changes hue.
Those who have hurt and those who have cried,
They rise and they aim and they carry on.
They are us.
It is the everydayness of bravery which inspires me.
My promise to myself is to carry on noticing these
offered things.
My task, to carry on gathering offered chances; set
awareness on: 'Receive'.

Living with a stalker

Dear Ray

I thought I would write this down while I am thinking about it – I should like to say it to you directly but you would probably "turn off" or try and change the subject so it's probably better written. I don't think you realise what a potentially dangerous state our relationship is in at the moment. I feel we are back on the road we were on prior to November 1995, and even if that hadn't happened, our relationship would have most certainly ended by now probably very bitterly and with a great deal of bad feeling. Leading up to that event was one of the most miserable periods of my life, and although at the moment it's nothing like as bad as then, I'm beginning to have times when that feeling comes back very strongly. Then, whenever you went out, I would wonder how drunk and how nasty you were going to be when you came back. If you were very drunk, you fell asleep quite soon, sometimes before being vile and abusive, but then there was the wet bed or sofa to contend with later.

If not too drunk I would usually have a worse time as it would be later before you went to sleep. I can't put into words how awful those times made me feel, and even though it was truly dreadful when you went to jail, the relief at not having to suffer your drunkenness anymore was a huge bonus.

Now I'm not saying for a minute that we have returned to that situation, but I do fear we are on the top of the road to it. When you go out now I have an anxiety in me that maybe you will have a drink (or a few drinks) and try to disguise it when you come home. Believe me you can't. I can tell when you've had a drink 95% of the time and I also know you lie to me. You're good at lying. Sometimes I'm sure you get away with it and I believe the crap you tell me, but sometimes I know you are lying.

The thing about drinking is I can't prove it. I'm, as I said 95% certain but there's always that little bit of doubt and if you swear blind (like you always do) that you haven't had a drink, I can't absolutely say you have. The trouble is that if this carries on, one day I *will* be able to prove it and that's where the end will come because we won't be able to pretend everything is okay anymore.

I don't want that to happen. I hope you don't either but I am beginning to wonder.

To go back a bit, when you first got out of jail I was full of hope for the future (I had lots of doubt and fears too but the hopes were far bigger). You seemed to have changed. You seemed to have got your priorities sorted out and you seemed a lot more focused and certainly more grown up (for want of a better word).

I was firstly very disappointed (and hurt) at the way our personal relationship developed, or rather didn't develop. I know I was a big turn off for you but it is hard to cope with the feeling of physical rejection especially when that used to be a big part of our life. But, rationally speaking I can't blame you for that one. I know what I look like and I hate myself for not being like I was before, so as I said, that one is my fault.

When you first went out on your own I obviously used to worry but after that first Christmas I began to relax thinking that you really had kicked the alcohol thing and it really didn't bother you anymore. Then we had all the nastiness in the autumn of last year and it took a while for me to realise that indeed the booze had reared its' ugly head again. All the signs were there, exactly the same patterns of behaviour and the dreaded awful feeling that I spoke of earlier came back again.

I was prepared for it to end and then you begged for 'one last chance'. You said you'd see an A.A Counsellor, which you never did and agreed to see the GP. Everything settled again, Christmas was fine and now four months on I'm seeing the signs on a few odd occasions. How long before those odd occasions become regular? How long then before we are right back to square one? Except it won't get that far again because we won't be together.

I want to state here and now that that I absolutely WILL NOT put up with that again. I have forgiven you for more things over the last twelve years than most people would do in a lifetime but this is the one thing that I won't forgive you for, if it ever comes to a final head. If you want to booze again I can't really stop you, but we won't be in a relationship together if you do.

I don't want to lose you. You have lots of good, kind and nice qualities. I can (I think) put up with your irresponsibility and your grumpiness because no one is perfect, but drinking is one I cannot and will not deal with. I don't want this letter to sound like a threat, it's just that I can't cope with the alcohol thing and if you have a brain and a conscience you will see that.

Drinking has been the root cause of all the bad things in your life and if that lesson hasn't sunk in by now then I fear it never will. So you had better have long hard think about things. If this is something you can't do then we had better end things here and now before they get bad and acrimonious.

It's really up to you Ray. I can't tell you what to do at the end of the day, but I can say what I am not prepared to live with, and you back on the booze (even mildly), is something I can't live with. Of course I may be assuming a lot here. Maybe you do really want to get out of this relationship and haven't got the guts to do it so by boozing again I kick you out and the problem is solved! After all I know you find my children difficult and my family, and even living in the village so perhaps it's all too much for you and as things are, I'm not enough to keep you here anymore.

All I'm saying is, if this is the case be honest about it. I wouldn't want you to stay if you weren't happy living here anymore. I would never try to make you stay. This is not saying I want you to go because I don't. I would be devastated for lots of reasons but I would eventually get over it. So you have a good think about what you want and try to be honest about it all. I don't believe in laying down the law but the only thing I'm asking of you is not to dally with alcohol again because I CANNOT cope with the consequences.

Please read this carefully a couple of times and let it sink in before you react because I mean every word, and you must believe that.

Dana

Stop Violence Against Women and Girls

Why VAWG should end?

Because 1-4 women will experience Domestic Violence in her lifetime . . . and I'm one of them.

Because 1-5 women will be a victim of rape or attempted rape in her lifetime . . . and I'm one of them.

VAWG must end because I'm just tired of being a statistic.

VAWG must end because the next number on my list, 2, is the number of women who are killed each week by a current or former partner. This means that one woman will be dead every three days . . . and I refuse to be one of them!

I see violence against women just like cancer in our society, it creeps in, and slowly metastasizes in our daily lives and takes its deadly toll without mercy, without stopping, without intermission, and it's not okay just to stand back and feel sorry for those affected, because just like cancer; the next victim could be you, your sister, your mother, your daughter, your best friend.

And let me ask you – what would you do if it gets any of them? I mean, how far would you go if violence of any kind (physical, emotional or psychological) hits your loved ones?

Would you then try to stop it?

I'm sure you would.

Then we must do something about it now, because domestic violence will touch your life or the life of someone you know at some point.

VAWG will succumb if we all - men and women, stand together in a strong coalition based on information, trust and dedication.

Alone we are tiny raindrops, that separated do not stand a chance, but together we are a powerful storm so strong that it is impossible to be contained.

Please be a raindrop in my rain of power to stop violence against women, so we shall live our lives through faith rather than in fear.

TRIVIALISING STALKING

"Often you don't know whether you're the hero of a romantic comedy or the villain on a Lifetime special until the restraining order arrives."

— Tim Kreider, *We Learn Nothing*

Coming forward
can be difficult in any
situation but is made
worse by a society
in which stalking is
often seen as
something of a joke
and is often
misunderstood by
the public and
professionals alike.

National Stalking Helpline

I AM NOT STALKING YOU!!!

By the way,
you're out of milk.

Relatable Post #1950

friend request accepted
Let the stalking begin

"
"Stalking" is such a
strong word, I prefer
"Intense Research of
an individual". "

Stalking – funny ha-ha? Or funny peculiar?

"I sneaked out to his house a couple times in the middle of the night to watch over him while he slept, just in case, I don't know, his comic book collection decided to spontaneously combust."

"Stalking is when two people go for a long romantic walk together but only one of them knows about it."

"I had taken the photograph from afar (distance being the basic glitch in our relationship), using my Nikon and zoom lens while hiding behind a fake marble pillar. I was hiding because if he knew I'd been secretly photographing him for all these months he would think I was immature, neurotic and obsessive.

I'm not.
I'm an artist.
Artists are always misunderstood.

(www.google.co.uk/funny+stalking+quotes)

PRACTICAL TIPS

"The best advice I ever got is that
knowledge is power and to keep reading."

— David Bailey

"Individual commitment to a group effort –
that is what makes a team work,
a company work,
a society work,
a civilization work."

— Vince Lombardi

STALKING FACTS

- Understanding the context of the stalking behaviours is crucial to effective safety planning and risk management.

- The majority of stalkers are known to their victims either as ex-partners or acquaintances, but some people are stalked by complete strangers.

- 1 in 10 domestic violence victims confide in a manager or work colleague (Roe 2010).

- Around 80% of stalkers are male. However, stalkers and their victims can be of either gender.

- Stalkers come from all backgrounds and do not form one 'type'. Stalkers are not homogenous and the motivation for stalking can vary.

- Understanding the motivation and context is important when assessing the risks that the stalker may pose.

- Many victims will experience multiple, repeated stalking behaviours before they report this to the police.

STALKING LEGISLATION

The Protection of Freedoms Act 2012 amended the Protection from Harassment Act 1997, to introduce two new offences of Stalking:

Section 2a: Prohibits a person from pursuing a course of conduct that amounts to Stalking and

Section 4a: Prohibits a person from pursuing a course of conduct that amounts to Stalking causing fear of violence or serious alarm or distress and has a substantial impact on the victim's day to day activities and which the perpetrator knows or ought the know amounts to Stalking.

Stalking is a two-part crime: that is characterised by an obsessive fixation of the stalker on their victim by repeatedly attempting to contact, call, text, follow, monitor online behaviour or impose any kind of unwanted communications on another person and those incidents form a pattern of behaviour.

When those behaviours are carried out in a manner that could be expected to cause distress or fear to any reasonable person; and the victims have had to significantly modify their lives, an offence of stalking has been committed.

To establish a course of conduct the behaviour has to occur on at least two occasions, due to the distressing nature of stalking, most perpetrators should be arrested and charged under section 4(a)

A recent Crime Survey of England and Wales shows that up to 700,000 women are stalked each year (2009-2012), 1 in 5 women and 1 in 10 men will experience stalking in their lifetime and the British Crime survey 2006 suggests that up 5,000,000 people are stalked each year.

STALKING IS A CRIME. REPORT IT!

DASH STALKING QUESTIONS

1. Is the victim very frightened?

2. Is there previous domestic abuse or harassment/stalking history?

3. Have they vandalised or destroyed property?

4. Have they turned up unannounced more than three times a week?

5. Have they followed the victim or loitered near their home or workplace?

6. Have they made threats of physical or sexual violence?

7. Have they harassed any third party since the harassment began?

8. Have they acted violently to anyone else during the stalking incident?

9. Have they engaged other people to help him/her?

10. Have they had problems in the past year with drugs (prescription or other), alcohol or mental health leading to problems in leading a normal life?

11. Have they ever been in trouble with the police or has a criminal history for violence or anything else?

PRACTICAL ADVICE FOR VICTIMS

- Report Stalking incidents to the police.

- Keep a diary of all incidents and how they made you feel.

- Keep you text messages, emails, objects and screenshots for evidence.

- Consider carrying a personal alarm.

- Vary your daily routine and take different routes to and from work.

- Know where the nearest safe location is, for instance a police station. But, if there isn't one nearby, you could use a 24-hour supermarket with security guards and CCTV cameras.

- Talk to the police about using CCTV and/or installing a panic button at your home.

- Ensure all your doors and windows are locked before you leave home or go to sleep.

- Do not engage with your stalker in any way.

- Talk to neighbours, colleagues and/or your line manager about the harassment if you feel comfortable doing so. They may be able to help by collecting further evidence on your behalf or by putting protective measures in place.

Paladin – National Stalking Advocacy Service

PRACTICAL ADVICE FOR ALL PROFESSIONALS

Stalking as a pattern of repeated and persistent behaviour that is intrusive and engenders fear. One person becomes fixated or obsessed with another and the attention is unwanted.

Stalking behaviour can be seen as unwanted communications, from telephone calls to messages or intrusions that include waiting for, spying on, approaching and entering a person's home. Additionally, the stalker may make complaints to legitimate bodies or use the Internet and social media to continue their campaign. Occasionally, they will make threats, damage property or use violence but even if there is no threat **stalking is still a crime**.

IF YOU SUPPORT VICTIMS

- Believe them and take them seriously.

- Ensure you listen carefully and record everything you are told.

- Record the extent of the victim's perception of risk of harm.

- Take disclosures of threats to kill seriously.

- If there has been a relationship, ask the victim to complete a DASH risk assessment and 11 stalking screening questions.

- If there has not been a relationship, ask the victim to complete the 11 risk screening questions.

- Ask if there is a restraining order.

- Ensure the victims keep a diary of all stalking incidents, retain all messages, gifts, etc.

- Seek specialist advice from your local police force. Each force has a Single Point of Contact or other units if required, such as the Public Protection Unit.

- Tell the victim to call the National Stalking Helpline on 0808 802 0300.

NEVER

- Never think it any less serious if there has been no physical violence.

- Never send the person away believing that it is not a serious or say that they are 'lucky' to receive this kind of attention.

- Never tell them to change their phone number. This will not stop the behaviour - they will find another means of contact.

- Never mediate or suggest that the victim talk/meet with the stalker to resolve issues.

Cyberstalking

**17% of the information that
stalkers find out about
their victims online come from
public records.**

University of Leicester/NSS survey, 2005

Understanding Cyberstalking

I have worked with Veritas for about a year now, and in that time I have met many people from varying backgrounds. My professional experience is in the field of security, now specialising in cyber security, so it became apparent that there was a demand for knowledge and advice on this subject within the organisation. It was inevitable, I feel, that the two of us would work together at some point.

Although Veritas focuses on all forms of stalking, cyberstalking was understood to be a fairly new crime, and it was this that was going to push my learning curve in a slightly different direction. With the advent of connected technology – the everyday devices we use that are almost permanently connected to the Internet – stalking has become that much more remote for the perpetrator. This allows them a perceived level of anonymity and a constant, unwanted presence in the life of their victim. As a result, tracing those committing this crime, and any cyber crimes for that matter, is an ongoing challenge for those of us involved in cyber security.

As with any security industry, the conflict between criminals and crime fighters is a metaphorical game of tennis. The crime is committed, a defence is installed and then that defence is breached. This then continues back and forth ad infinitum. The winner is whomever happens to be ahead at that point in time, and if that happens to be the criminal then it's up to the authorities to pick up the pieces in the pursuit of justice.

With stalking, those affected by a perpetrator's campaign often don't associate the behaviour with stalking or realise that it is a criminal offence. It is only when supporting professionals become involved that the actions seem remarkable. I use the word 'campaign' simply because stalkers are, by the very definition, obsessively focussed on their main objective: to cause distress and fear to the victim, and disrupt their life by unwanted repeated contact, sometimes including acts of physical violence.

Technology has become an incredibly useful tool in this campaign, and perpetrators will learn, either online or, ironically, in custodial rehabilitation classes, to utilise hardware and software in order to reach their goals. Other than the easy and abundant communication options offered with social media and many instant messaging applications, not to mention the now almost 'antique' methods of simple SMS texting and phone calls, I think that the main benefit of mobile devices to stalkers is location tracking. Connected devices are now all fitted with some way of transmitting their location to within a few metres, and to a stalker that is valuable information. It is imperative that anyone who suspects that their devices may have been compromised take a very close look at their own and their family's location settings on every connected device in their life. If necessary, seek professional advice from a qualified specialist or technician.

The topic of cyber security is very current and we see reports both online and in the printed and televised media of data breaches far more often. However, there is a skills gap in this field like no other that I have seen, simply because there is a virtual war breaking out with viral speed. Cyber security is a specialised area and the knowledge-base is vast. There is so much cyber news to keep up with on a daily basis that I have had to abandon all other news in order to have time in the day to complete actual work.

This, then, gives me some concern over the current levels of support and resources that the Police Service has been allocated in both its UK cyber headquarters and around the country, along with the current level of training that staff are given to deal with the offences that the national security services don't deal with. If one adds cyberstalking into the mix with online fraud, identity theft and other crimes, victims of stalking may not be getting the level of support that they need *when* they need it. And with a crime such as stalking, time really is of the essence. The Police Service are working on a programme to train more staff to a high level of cyber crime awareness and qualification in order to ensure that the UK has sufficient coverage. However, this will take another 2-3 years to reach full capability.

It is time to readdress the myth that stalking perpetrators are lower risk offenders based on a lack of proximity or physical violence, and that abuse *can* still escalate to potentially tragic consequences. Lessons are all very well, but how many lessons are needed before preventative measures are taken without haste?

Technically average perpetrators are becoming advanced users in order to meet their goals. It is only right, then, that those looking for the perpetrators, and supporting those affected by stalking campaigns, do likewise and become fully aware of online technology, its vulnerabilities and how to manage the sharing of private information in order to reduce the risk to personal safety. These huge advances in technology and connectivity should be working in the authorities' favour in this fight, with proper secure online incident logging for victims, reviewed by a single point-of-contact at the local Police station. Only that way can events be assessed properly, flagged up and investigated as priority actions and evidence be clearly logged for future use.

While Veritas has made, and continues to make, fantastic progress since its launch, there is still much to be done, particularly in terms of partnership work. The organisation is committed to offering support to service users, whilst also providing training to professionals based on the unique approach of using both academic and personal experience. In addition, there is a constant need for the application of pressure in the pursuit of legal and political reform, and publicity for a crime which, by all accounts, is still widely ignored or trivialised. I get great satisfaction from helping people, but helping people who are desperately in need of it has no equal.

Nick Podd

TIPS TO STAY SAFE ONLINE

With more than 10 billion connected devices on the planet at this current time, and that figure set to rise exponentially, it is little wonder that our digital footprints are growing at an equal rate.

If you are worried about your online presence and/or privacy, and would like to take decisive action to lower the risks, there are a number of ways that you can do this.

SECURITY - DON'T

- Do not use password names or words that can be found in the dictionary, however long. These **can** be cracked, with the correct software and knowledge, in seconds.

- Do not pick easy security questions or use answers that people will know. If everyone you know knows the town in which you were born, consider using a more obscure piece of information.

- Never leave your devices unattended, unless you are at home and feel safe, whether they are locked or not. With today's sophisticated software, information can be extracted from your device and tracking apps can be installed without your knowledge.

- Never open email attachments from anyone that you do not recognise. They could well be executable files (a file that will run a process when opened) that will install malware (viruses, Trojans, spyware, rootkits, bots, keyloggers etc.) into your computer or device. Although viruses are the most commonly discussed form of malware, they are low on the list of distributed attacks. Trojans, malicious applications that allow criminals to remotely access your computer, are by far the most common form of malware.

SECURITY - DO

- ALWAYS use strong passwords – use a combination of upper and lower case letters, numbers and, for added security, special characters (e.g. !@£$%^&*<>?/ etc.)

- Where offered, ALWAYS activate two-factor authentication. This is a two-step security process involving something you know (e.g. a password) and something you have (e.g. a smartphone). Some online banks use this method with an issued keypad device or card reader, and some websites send temporary codes either via text to your phone or within their mobile app.

- If security questions are asked in the setting up of accounts, choose the most obscure questions or make up the answers. There is no law that states you have to tell the truth in answering these questions; they are simply to determine your identity.

- Keep all of your devices locked with a PIN or password when you are not using then. The more complicated the better.

- Most web browsers (for example, Internet Explorer/Edge, Mozilla Firefox, Google Chrome, Safari etc.) will have the facility of asking to save passwords for you. It is advisable to switch this function off in all cases, and certainly never accept the offer when on any other computer or device than your own.

- Always install reputable anti-malware applications on computers (sold in shops as anti-virus software packages) and keep them updated. It is wise to seek impartial advice on the best packages, as those included with new computers are not necessarily the best options. Software of this kind can also slow your computer down considerably, so take that into consideration.

- Look for the tell tale signs in emails – spelling errors, poor grammar, poor logos and so on. No financial institution or any commercial company will send an attachment without your prior knowledge. And no website will ever ask you to click on a link from an email to log in to your account. If in doubt, contact the company directly using the details on their website. **Always mark suspicious emails as SPAM** – this helps email providers with future filtering.

PRIVACY - DON'T

- Unless absolutely necessary (i.e. during the application process for a legal document or financial contract), do not disclose personal information about yourself, such as your date of birth, your personal or work addresses, or phone numbers and email addresses.

- Offer information of your whereabouts to anyone, unless you see fit to do so on rare occasions. For instance, you may be on holiday and wish to check in at a world famous landmark as a memory of your adventure. Be careful about telling people online and on social media sites where you are, especially if you are in a vulnerable situation.

- Always check the apps and browsers that you install on your devices and computers. Many will track you for the purposes of marketing and advertising, and you have the option to change the default settings and opt out. These apps can be adjusted in the settings area of your mobile device. There are also web browser extensions (bolt-on bits of software) that can be downloaded for free, which will prevent adverts from being displayed. It is worth searching for these options.

PRIVACY – DO

- If you suspect that you are being tracked by an individual, then disconnect your devices from any network connections. This will include WiFi connections and cellular data connections. Cellular or mobile data connections are the ways in which mobile devices send or receive data (such as web pages, images, videos clips, communicating via apps etc.) when no WiFi signal is being used. The connection will be indicated at the top of the device screen as one of the following, in order of speed: GPRS, EDGE (or E), 2G, 3G or 4G. 5G will be arriving shortly. This facility can be switched off in the settings area of your device.

- **All mobile devices come with location services – check these settings and know exactly what you are agreeing to.** Even your photographs will be subject to geotagging, being embedded with metadata that you can't see but will identify exactly where the photo was taken.

- Use disposable email addresses or aliases. You can get an email address from Google, Yahoo! and many others in minutes, and it is useful to have a gender neutral email address that you can use for anything that you may want to walk away from in the future, leaving no trace. You simply delete the account.

- Start using search engines that don't track everything that you do (e.g. duckduckgo.com). There are web browsers that offer less tracking too.

- Make sure that if you use social and business networking sites (such as Facebook, Twitter, Google+, LinkedIn, Instagram, Pinterest etc.) that you carefully check the security and privacy settings.

- Think carefully before you check in on social networking sites. Is it necessary to let people know that you are having coffee at a particular high street coffee chain in London? Information spreads quickly, even if your privacy settings are watertight.

- It's an idea to search for any details about yourself online on a regular basis, using any of the search engines. If details exist that you wish to be removed, then you can contact the webmaster at the relevant website (there will always be a link or address somewhere, usually at the bottom of the homepage) and ask for this to be done.

- Get yourself removed from contact detail data warehouse 192.com by going to their website and filling in the relevant form.

- Likewise, you may request to have your name removed from the Electoral Register by contacting your local council. However, be aware that this may have an effect on your credit score, voting and local authority identification.

- **Keep your security information secure.** Don't share it with anyone, whether you trust them or not. It is your information and yours alone. If you forget a password, there are procedures (in virtually all cases) for resetting it.

IF YOU SUSPECT THAT YOUR ACCOUNT OR DEVICE HAS BEEN COMPROMISED

A compromise may not necessarily mean that your account has been hacked. It may just mean that someone you know has gained access to your account via another means, either by guessing a password that you have often used, or by physically accessing one of your devices. In any case, take the following action:

- Change your password immediately.

- Contact the administrators of the website and inform them of the compromise. All social network sites have a 'Help' section that will direct you to the correct area.

- If the compromise is part of an ongoing campaign to harass or stalk you, then **report it to the Police**. All events must be reported as soon as possible so that action can be taken.

- If you think that your computer or handheld device has been compromised in any way, and that tracking or spy software may have been installed, then take it to a fully qualified and registered device engineer. If possible, find one on recommendation. If not, then use one of the well-known impartial rating websites to find a specialist with a high feedback rating. They will be able to investigate and clean your device for you. Make sure that anything found is logged for the Police.

Nick Podd
Cyber Security Specialist

Organisational Commitment

Training must become a day-to-day practice to ensure that victims are given the correct advice and support and stalkers are placed at the centre of the investigation more robust understanding of the complexities of stalking is required by communities as a whole.

It is time that stalking is no longer trivialized and misunderstood and the voices of all of those victimised by it are equally valued, respected as the basis for improving practices and outcomes.

Contributors

Susan Ardley
Olivia Banks
Trisha Bernal
Anusree Biswas Sasidharan
Maura Cowen
Indy Dhuga
Claudia Miles
Clair Morrow
Nick Podd
Gabby Price
Paola Rahme Morales
Naomi Stanley
Jo Stubbs
Sam Taylor
Annie Vince
Sandra Ward
Diane Wells
Sandra Ward
Diane Wells

Some names in this book have been changed to protect identities

Index

Writers	Pages

Photos	Pages
Nick Podd	Cover, 7, 47
Paola Rahme Morales	40
Kiran Sasidharan	41, 89
Indy Dhuga	63
Clare Bernal – **Courtesy of Trisha Bernal**	71
Claudia Miles	55, 95
Sam Taylor	16, 99

Useful Contacts

Sussex Police
Tel: 999 for emergency calls or 101 for non-emergencies
Web: www.sussex.police.uk

Veritas Justice CIC (Training, Support and Advice)
Tel: 07736 149940 or 07736 149960
Email: info@veritas-justice.co.uk
Web: www.veritas-justice.co.uk

Victim Support
Tel: 0808 16 89 111
Email: supportlineemail@victimsupport.org.uk
Web: www.victimsupport.org.uk

Paladin Service (National Stalking Advocacy Service)
Tel: 020 7840 8960
Email: info@paladinservice.co.uk
Web: www.paladinservice.co.uk

National Stalking Helpline
Tel: 0808 802 0300
Web: www.stalkinghelpline.org
Email: advice@stalkinghelpline.org

RISE (Refuge, Information, Support and Education)
Tel: 01273 622 822
Web: www.rise.org.uk

Protection Against Stalking (PAS)
Email: info@protectionagainststalking.org
Web: www.protectionagainststalking.org

Survivors Network (Supporting Survivors of Sexual Violence and Abuse)
Tel: Helpline - 01273 720110 (open 7pm – 9pm)
Email: Help@survivorsnetwork.org.uk
Web: survivorsnetwork.org.uk

NSPCC
Tel: 0808 800 5000
Email: help@nspcc.org.uk
Web: www.nspcc.org.uk